The
Try Not To
Laugh Challenge

300 Fun and Silly For Kids and Family

Dad Jokes Edition

Riddleland

~Dedicated~

To all the fathers and grandfathers

around the world

For being

The Biggest Hero to your sons

and

The First Love to your daughters

Table of Contents

Introduction

"The greatest gift my dad gave me was his sense of humor" ~ Bella Connors

We would like to personally thank you for purchasing this book. **The Try Not to Laugh Challenge: Dad Jokes Edition** is a very special edition that is close and dear to my heart. Our childhoods was filled with funny, silly and corny jokes. Some were even terrible. Our dads were trying to develop the sense of humor in us . They always say, "When we have a sense of humor, we look at the bright side of life." They also mentioned that one of the most important life skills is the ability to make someone we love to crack up laughing. So besides telling jokes, we also mastered the art of making silly faces and noises. This book is collection of jokes that our dad had with we as well as ones we picked up along parenthood to share with our children.

Like our other "Try Not To Laugh Challenge" books, this book is not meant to be read alone, but instead it is a game to be played with siblings, friends, family or between two people that would like to prove who is a better comedian. **May this book create many fun memories to you and your family.**

These jokes are written to be fun and easy to read. Children learn best when they are playing. Reading can help increase that vocabulary and comprehension. They have also many other benefits such as:

- **Bonding** – It is an excellent way for parents and their children to spend some quality time and create some fun and memorable memories.

- **Confidence Building** - When parents give the riddles, it creates a safe environment for children to burst out answers even if they are incorrect. This helps the children to develop self confidence in expressing themselves.

- **Improve Vocabulary** – Jokes are usually written in easy to advance words, therefore children will need to understand these words before they can share the jokes.

- **Better reading comprehension** – Many children can read at a young age but may not understand the context of the sentences. Riddles can help develop the children's interest to comprehend the context before they can share it to their friends.

- **Sense of humor** –Funny creative jokes can help children develop their sense of humor while getting their brains working.

Rules of the Game!

The Goal is to make your opponent laugh

- Face your opponent.
- Stare at them!
- Make funny faces and noises to throw your opponent off
- Take turns reading the jokes out loud to each other
- When someone laughs, the other person wins a point

First person to get 5 points, is crowned The Champion!

Alert: Bonus Book for the Kids!

https://bit.ly/riddlelandbonus

Thank you for buying this book, We would like to share a special bonus as a token of appreciation. It is collection 50 original jokes, riddles and 2 funny stories

RIDDLES AND JOKES CONTESTS!!

Riddleland is having **2 contests** to see who are the smartest or funniest boys and girls in the world.

1) **Creative and Challenging Riddles**
2) **Tickle Your Funny Bone Contest**

Parents, please email us your child's "Original" Riddle or Joke **and he or she could win a $50 gift card to Amazon. Here are the rules:**

1) It must be challenging for the riddles and funny for the jokes!
2) It must be 100% Original and not something from the internet! It is easy to find out!
3) You can submit both joke and riddle as they are 2 separate contests.

4) No help from the parents unless they are as funny as you.

5) Winners will be announced via email.

6) Email us at <u>Riddleland@bmccpublishing.com</u>

Other Fun Children Books for The Kids!

Riddles Series

Encourage your kids to think outside of the box

with these Fun and Creative Riddles!

Get them on Amazon!

Try Not to Laugh Challenge Series

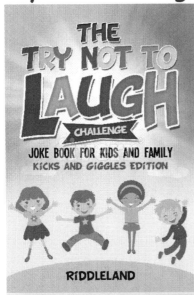

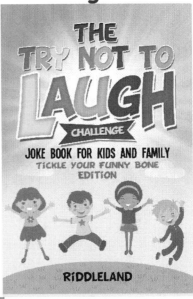

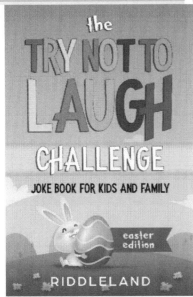

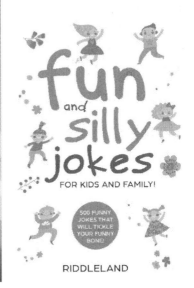

Get them on Amazon!

Chapter 1: Dad's Q&A Challenge

Parenting is saying the same thing *over* and *over* and expecting *different results*. Oddly enough, that is the definition of *insanity*. Coincidence? I think not!

~ Anonymous

1) What's black and white and read all over?

A newspaper!

2) What's black and white, black and white, black and white?

A penguin rolling down a hill!

3) What's black and white and goes round and round?

A penguin in the washing machine.

4) What do you call a parrot at the North Pole?

Lost!

5) What do you call a boomerang that doesn't come back?

A stick!

6) Why can't the baby horse sing?

Because it's a little hoarse.

7) What do you do if you think there's something in your shoe?

Check to see if it's your foot.

8) What kind of books do owls like to read?

Hoot-dunnits.

9) Why are false teeth like stars?

Because they come out at night!

10) What did the banana say to the dog?

Nothing – bananas can't talk!

11) What did the snowman say to his friend?

Do you smell carrots

12) What kind of sandals do toads wear?

Open toad.

13) Why did Rachel's dad throw her clock out of the window?

Because he wanted to see time fly!

14) What is a computer's favorite snack?

Computer chips!

15) What's brown, hairy and wears sunglasses?

A coconut on vacation!

16) What do you call a three-legged donkey?

A wonkey!

17)**What do you call a hot Daddy snowman?**

Water

18) **What do you call a parrot wearing earmuffs?**

Anything you like – he can't hear you!

19) **What did the American chimpanzee wave on Flag Day?**

A star-spangled banana!

20) **What do you call two people who embarrass you at your Parents' Evening?**

Mom and Dad!

21) **What's the best thing about school?**

The vacations!

22) **What's the difference between a teacher and a book?**

You can shut a book up.

22) What did the hat say to the scarf?

You hang around and I'll go on ahead.

23) What do you get if you cross a kangaroo with a sheep?

A woollen jumper!

24) What do you give a sick pig?

OINKment!

25) Where do cows go to see a film?

To the moo-vies!

26) What do you get if you multiply 5,482 by 3,458, and then divide the answer by 64?

A bad headache!

27) Which is the fruitiest lesson you get at school?

History, because it's full of dates!

28) Do you know what an alligator's favorite card game is?

Snap!

29) What flies through the air with a terrible smell?

A smelly-copter!

30) What did the shy pebble say?

I wish I was a little boulder.

31) Why did the helicopter land outside your bedroom?

I must have left the landing light on!

32) Why did the one-eyed principal have to close his school?

He only had one pupil!

33) Why was the math book so sad?

Because he had too many problems.

34) Why is the sky so high?

So, the birds don't bump their heads.

35) What do you call a cow that eats the grass in your yard?

A lawn-mooer!

36) Why did the bald man paint rabbits all over his head?

Because from a distance they looked like hares!

37) How did the ringmaster start his flea circus?

One, two, flea...go!

38) What do moths study at school?

Mothomatics!

39) Why did the golfer wear two pairs of trousers?

In case he got a hole in one!

40) What did the cookie say when he got run over?

Oh crumbs!

41) What's grey with a trunk?

A mouse going on holiday.

42) What's brown with a trunk?

The same mouse coming back from holiday.

43) What do you do if you find a gorilla sitting at your desk in school?

Move to a different desk.

44) What do you give sick birds?

Tweetment.

45) What has an elephant's trunk, a tiger's paws, a giraffe's neck and a chimpanzee's bottom?

A zoo.

46) What goes zzub, zzub?

A bee flying backwards!

47) Why are pirates called pirates?

Because they aaarrrr!

48) What do you call a bee, if it's always grumbling?

A grumble bee!

49) Why don't baby birds ever smile?

Would you like it if your mother fed you worms every day?

50) Why do humming birds hum?

Because they never learn the words to the songs!

51) What are an alien's favorite candies?

Martian-mallows.

52) What does an Australian witch ride on?

A broomerang.

53) What happened to the naughty chicken at school?

He got eggspelled.

54) Which snake is best at math?

The adder.

55) What did the nose shout when he went to audition

for the school play?

Pick me! Pick me!

56) What did one trashcan say to another trashcan?

"Put a lid on it!"

57) What is a frog's favorite flower?

The croak-us.

58) What's a monster's favorite soup?

Scream of tomato.

59) Which bus crossed the Atlantic Ocean?

Christopher Colum-bus.

60) What would a kind alien say when it met you for the first time?

Pleased to meteor you!

61) What would an unkind alien say when he met you for the first time?

Pleased to eat you!

62) What sort of dog has no tail?

A hot dog.

63) Why is the sky so high?

So the birds don't bang their heads.

64) What do you call a sleeping bull?

A bulldozer.

65) What do snowmen wear on their heads?

Ice caps.

66) How do fleas travel?

They go itch-hiking.

67) Where does the king keep his armies?

Up his sleevies!

68) What do snowmen call their sons and daughters?

Chill-dren.

69) What do you get when you cross a dinosaur with fireworks?

Dinomite.

70) Why do giraffes have long necks?

Because their feet smell.

71) How do sheep celebrate their birthdays?

They sing "Happy birthday to ewe".

72) What would you get if you crossed a skunk with a sheep?

I don't know, but it would smell really baaad.

73) What has four wheels and flies?

A dustcart!

74) How does a chicken tell the time?

One o'cluck, two o'cluck,,,,

75) What sort of cat always knows which way to go?

A compuss.

76) Which vegetable should you never take on a cruise?

A leek.

77) What sort of stones are never found in the ocean?

Dry ones.

78) What do you find in a small ocean?

Micro-waves.

79) Why are aliens so forgetful?

Because everything they hear goes in one ear and out of all the others.

80) Where do otters come from?

Otter space.

81) Where does a Dutch hamster come from?

Hamsterdam!

82) Why was the mommy centipede so upset?

Because all of her kids needed new shoes!

83) What do bees comb their hair with?

A honeycomb

84) What do you call a hamster with a top hat?

Abrahamster Lincoln.

85) What leans to one side and has a cheese and tomato topping?

The Leaning Tower of Pizza.

86) Where do toads keep their treasure?

In a croak of gold at the end of a rainbow.

87) What is the fastest vegetable?

A runner bean.

88) What would you say to a frog who needed a lift?

"Hop in!"

89) What do you call a fish that's eaten 24 carrots?

A goldfish.

90) How did the computer criminal get out of jail?

He pressed the escape key.

91) What sort of music are balloons afraid of?

Pop music.

92) Why isn't it safe to make jokes when you're ice skating?

Because the ice might crack up!

93) What do double agents play when they go on holiday?

I spy.

94) Why is a tomato round and red?

Because if it was long and green it would be a cucumber.

95) What do you call a monster with no neck?

The Lost Neck Monster.

96) What do lions call antelopes?

Fast food.

97) What happens when you cut three oranges, four pears and six bananas into ten pieces each?

A fruit salad!

98) What bird can pick up heavy objects?

A crane!

Chapter 2 - Animal Jokes

"My father used to play with my brother and me in the yard. Mother would come out and say, "You're tearing up the grass." "We're not raising grass," Dad would reply. "We're raising boys." ~ Harmon Killebrew

1) At the restaurant, Dad asked for French toast and bacon.

"How do you like your French toast?" asked the waiter.

"I don't know," replied Dad. "You haven't brought it over yet."

2) The daddy spider watched his son, tapping away on his computer.

"Son," he said, "you're spending too much time on the web."

3) "Dad," said Bella, "Can you tell me a joke, please?"

"Sure," said Dad. Then he frowned. "I thought I knew a good joke about a boomerang," he said, "but I've forgotten it." Then his eyes lit up.

"Wait a minute," he said, "I think it's coming back to me...."

4) Bella asked her dad to tell her another joke.

Dad thought for a moment.

"I think I know one about a ceiling," he said.

"It's not the best joke in the world but it's up there!"

5) Mia skipped up to her Dad.

"I know some jokes about golf," Mia told him.

"Join the club!" said Dad.

6) Daddy Strawberry was crying. "Boo hoo!" he sobbed.

"Why are you crying, dear?" asked Mommy Strawberry.

"Because we're in a jam!" replied Daddy Strawberry.

7) Lucy and her father snuggled together on the sofa.

"Hey Pops, will you tell me a story, please?" asked Lucy.

"Sure, Lucy" said her father. "I'd tell you the one about a broken pencil, but it'd be pointless."

8) It was bedtime, and time for a story.

"Daddy, will you think up a story about a giant for me?" asked Jamie.

"Sure," said her father, "but I'll have to use big words."

9) It was a sunny day and Cassie wanted a story.

"Hey Dad, do you know any stories about orange juice?" she asked.

"I'm sure I can think of one," said her dad, "but I'll have to concentrate!"

10) "What shall we read for tonight's bedtime story?"
asked Ricky.

"How about this book about the history of glue?"
suggested his dad.

"I just can't put it down!"

11) Dad's nose was stuck in a book. "What are you
reading?" asked Ava.

"This is a great book about the history of ship building,"
replied Dad.

"Shall I read it to you? It's riveting!"

12) Dad and Luke were enjoying a picnic together.
"Err....Luke," said Dad, watching his son eat an apple,
"do you know what's worse than finding a worm in that
apple that you're eating?"

"Finding two worms, perhaps?" suggested Luke.

"No," replied Dad. "Finding half a worm!"

13) "Look at that sale," said Mom. "They have a TV for just five dollars, but the volume is stuck on full." "Five dollars?" said Dad.

"For that price you just can't turn it down!"

14) Archie watched as his father loaded a ladder onto the roof of their car. "Why are you taking that ladder to parents' night, Dad?" he asked.

"It's obvious, son," came he replied. "Because you told me you wanted to go to high school."

15) Dad was wearing sunglasses, even though it was dark outside.

"Why are you wearing sunglasses to my parents' evening, Dad?" asked Jack.

"Because the kids in your class are all so bright!" said his dad.

16) Dad was talking to the Principal at Emily's school.

"Do you know how many teachers work at this school?"

asked the Principal.

"I'd say about half of them!" said Emily's dad.

17) "I've just had a terrible fright," said Sarah's dad at

Parents' Evening. "The school janitor just jumped out of a

cupboard!"

Sarah's teacher looked puzzled. "Oh! What did he say?" she

asked.

"Supplies, supplies!" said Dad.

18) Dave came back from the hospital with his arm in

plaster.

"I've broken my arm in several places," he told his Dad.

"Well, don't go to those places again."

19) My dad went to the doctor. He said, "Doctor, I feel like a bridge." "What's went over you?" asked the doctor.

"Two cars, a truck and a bus," said my dad.

20) "Your jokes are terrible, Dad," said Paula.

"Can you think of a funny one for a change?"

"Have I told you that joke about the roof?" asked Dad.

"I don't think so..." "Never mind," said Dad. "I think it's over your head!"

21) Lyla's dad came home from work looking sad. "I've decided to give up my job in the can-crushing factory," he told his daughter.

"Why is that, Dad?" Lyla asked.

Dad sighed. "It was soda pressing."

22) Dad went into a pet shop to buy a goldfish.

"Do you want an aquarium?" asked the pet shop owner.

"I don't mind what star sign it is," said Dad.

23) Eddie walked into the kitchen. His father was eating one of his school books! "That's my homework, Dad!" he cried.

"Why are you eating it?"

"Because you told me it's a piece of cake!" said Dad.

24) "Hey Dad," said Mike. "Do you know any jokes about pizza?"

Dad thought for a moment.

"Well..." he said, "I did hear one once, but it was too cheesy."

25) "For homework I have to think of three sentences using the word "beans"," said Ellie. "We grow beans in the garden," said Mom.

"Uncle Arnie cooks beans," said Ronnie.

Dad spoke up next. "We are all human beans," he said.

26) It was 7am and Dan's tummy was rumbling.

"Hey Dad," he said, "it's your turn to cook breakfast,
isn't it?"

Dad was already heading for the kitchen.

"Of course, it is," he said. "It's Fryday!"

27) Simon ran over to his father.

"Dad! Dad!" he cried, "I keep seeing insects circling
around the room!"

Dad just carried on reading his newspaper.

"Don't worry, son," he replied. "There's a bug going around."

28) Paula wanted to tell her dad her favorite joke.

"Dad! Dad!" she said, "what kind of shoes do you make
out of banana skins?"

Dad was ready with the answer. "Slippers!" he grinned.

29) Felicity was looking sad.

She tugged at her father's arm as he worked on his computer. "Dad! Dad!" she sighed.

"I keep thinking I'm a pair of drapes!"

Dad was busy. "You need to pull yourself together, my dear," he replied.

30) It was a winter's day and Dad came in from the yard soaked to the skin. "Kids! I just fell through the ice on our pond.

I think I've become a POPsicle!" he shivered.

31) Jenny and her dad were birdwatching together. Dad pointed at a tiny wren. "Why is that baby bird just like me, Jenny?" he asked. "I don't know, Dad," said Jenny, "but I'm sure you're going to tell me..." Dad smiled.

"It's because he's a CHIRP off the old block!" he replied.

32) Tracy is almost eight years old. She'd been

thinking... "Hey Dad," she said,

"I'd love to have a space party for my next birthday."

Dad liked the idea. "No problem," he said, "but we'll have to

planet early!"

33) "Mark had a frown on his face. He turned to his

father.

"Why is my teacher cross-eyed, Dad?" he asked.

"I know why - he can't control his pupils," grinned Dad.

34) Dad was with his kids at the restaurant.

He pushed his plate away from him and called the

waitress over. "Do you know how many rotten eggs there

were in that omelet?" he asked.

"Quite a phew," she replied.

34) Brandon woke up one morning to find his dad measuring his bed.

"What *are* you doing, Dad?" he asked.

"I just wanted to find out how long you'd slept," replied Dad.

35) The toy bear family was out at a restaurant.

Daddy Bear shook his head when offered a dessert.

"It's not like you to say 'no' to dessert, Daddy Bear," said Mommy Bear.

"Yeah, I know," sighed Daddy Bear, "but I'm stuffed."

36) Chuck brought home his school report.

"Look, Dad," he said with a grin on his face. "I got straight As."

"Just think," said Dad. "If you were a duck, I could call you a wise quacker."

37) Barnie pushed away his plate, looking a little green.

"I wish I hadn't eaten that seafood," he groaned.

"Why not?" asked Dad, still munching away.

"Are you feeling a little eel?"

38) "I'm *sooo* tired," said Jack.

"Go and run around your bed for a while," suggested

Dad.

"It's a good way to catch up on your sleep!"

39) "Ring ring!" went the phone.

Chris picked up the receiver. "Who's speaking, please?"

he asked.

"You are, son," came Dad's voice at the other end of the line.

40) Connor's dad is a doctor. Once he had a patient

who'd had a serious accident. The patient shouted,

"Doctor, doctor, I can't feel my legs!"

Connor's Dad replied, "I know you can't - I've cut off your

arms!"

41) Jacob's Dad once met the man who invented crosswords. "I can't remember what his name was," he told Jacob.

"It was P something T something R..."

42) "Where can I get a potato clock?" asked Dad.

"Why do you need a potato clock?" wondered Mom.

"Well," said Dad, "my new boss told me I need to get a-potato-clock!"

43) Sophia the snake looked worried.

"Dad, are we poisonous?" she asked.

"Yes, Sophia, we are," he told her. "Why do you ask?"

"Because I just bit my tongue," said Sophia.

44) "Dinner's on me!" said Mom at the restaurant.

"No, it's not," said Dad. "It's on your plate!"

45) Dad was wandering round a gift store.

"I'm trying to buy a birthday present for my daughter," he said to the store assistant. "Can you help me out?"

"Sure," said the store assistant. "Which way did you come in?"

46) "Dad," said Leo one evening, "do you think people should be punished for something they haven't done?" "Of course not, Leo," said Dad.

"Oh that's good," said Leo. "I haven't done my homework."

47) A man walks into a library and asks for a burger with fries.

The librarian says, "Sorry, sir, this is a library".

"Oh," replies the man (in a whisper), "Sorry, a burger with fries, please".

48) "Dad, what do you call that insect standing guard outside your bedroom door?" asked Mollie.

"A sentry-pede," said Dad.

49) "Why did the chicken cross the road?" asked Dad.

"I don't know," said Jessica.

"To get to the shop," laughed Dad.

"Did you think that was funny?" asked Jessica.

"Because I didn't."

"No, neither did the chicken," said Dad, "because the shops

were shut!"

50) "Did you hear about hairdressers?" said Dad to Mom.

"They aren't cutting hair any longer!" "Really?" said

Mom. "I can't believe it!"

Dad smirked. "No," he said. "They're cutting it shorter!"

51) Dad gave Cliff a tiny, tiny present for his birthday.

"You know, son, that it's the thought that counts?" said

his Dad.

Cliff sighed. "Couldn't you have some thoughts that were a

little bit bigger?"

52) "For your birthday," announced Dad, "I've baked you a cake filled with baked beans." "That sounds disgusting," said Richard. "Yes," said Dad. "But it'll mean you have a birthday cake that blows out its own candles."

53) "Time for your bedtime story," said Dad to Lucca. "Great!" said Lucca. "Can we have a story about a dragon?" "Of course," said Dad.
"Once upon a time there was a dragon. In a terrible battle, he pulled a knight in shining armor from his horse. With his mighty teeth, he bit into the knight, but then spat him out again in disgust." "Why did he do that?" asked Lucca.
"Because he didn't like canned food," said Dad.

54) Justin was in a bad mood. "Hey, Justin," said Dad, "do you know what's big and green and sits in the corner looking as miserable as you do?" "No," sighed Justin.
"The incredible sulk!"

55) Dad went to the doctor on Monday.

He said, "Doctor, I feel like a pack of cards."

"I'll deal with you later," said the doctor.

56) Dad went to the doctor on Tuesday.

"Doctor, Doctor," he said. "I feel like a biscuit."

"You must be crackers," said the doctor.

57) Dad went to the doctor on Wednesday.

"Doctor, Doctor," he said. "I think I need glasses."

"You certainly do," came the answer. "This is a hardware

store!"

58) Dad went to the doctor on Thursday.

"Doctor, Doctor," he said. "I feel like I'm shrinking."

"Well, said the doctor, "you'll have to be a little patient,

then."

59) Dad went to the doctor on Friday.

"Doctor, Doctor," he said. "I can't get to sleep at night."

"Lie on the edge of the bed," said the doctor. "You'll soon drop off."

60) "I can jump higher than a house!" said Dad.

Rob shook his head. "No you can't," he said.

"Yes I can, son," said Dad, "and I bet you $100 that I can..." "OK," said Rob. "Show me."

Dad did a little jump in the air. "See" he said.

"I told you I could jump higher than a house... Houses can't jump!"

61) "Doctor doctor, I think I'm an apple!" said Dad.

"Well come over here," said the doctor. "I won't bite you."

62) "Doctor doctor, I keep seeing double!" said Dad.

"Well come and sit down on the couch," said the doctor.

"Yes, but which one?"

63) Freddie was doing his history homework. He sighed.

"I wish I'd been born hundreds of years ago," he said.

"Then I'd have far less history to learn about."

64) "I remember writing poetry at school," said Dad.

"I wasn't very good at it.

None of my poems rhymed, and when we had to write a

sonnet,

things went from bad to verse!"

65) Noah's class was learning about American

Independence. "Can you tell me what happened at the

Boston Tea Party?" she asked.

"I have no idea, Miss," said Noah. "I wasn't invited."

66) Gabriel was watching two fleas playing soccer in a

saucer.

"What are they doing?" asked Dad.

"They're practicing for the cup," said Gabriel.

67) Dad was at the restaurant.

"Waiter," he said, "I can't eat this soup.

It's disgusting! Fetch me the manager."

"It's no use," said the waiter," he won't eat it, either."

68) At the restaurant, Dad had to call the waiter over.

"Waiter," he said, "what kind of soup is this?"

"It's bean soup, sir," replied the waiter.

"I don't care what it's been; what is it now?"

69) "I know a really great insect joke," said Dad.

"Can you tell it to me?" asked Harper. Dad thought for a

moment.

"Oh dear – I've forgotten the punchline, and it's really

bugging me."

70) Grandpa steam train was looking after the baby train. But the poor baby train wasn't feeling too well. He had a bad cold and kept sneezing.

"Oh dear!" said Grandpa.

"I think we'll have to call you achoo-choo train from now on."

71) "When I grow up," said the garbage man, "I want to be a dancer." "Why's that?" asked his dad.

"So that I can do the can-can!"

72) Amy went to school on Tuesday with glue smeared all over her head.

"Why on earth did you do that?" asked her teacher.

"I thought it would help things stick in my mind," replied Amy.

73) "I've just been to the doctor's" said Lazy Lionel. "He says I can't play football."

"Oh," said his teacher, "so he's seen you play, too, has he?"

74) "I need to find out the name of a deadly poison for my science project," said Lewis. "Parachuting," said Dad. "Parachuting?" said Lewis. "That's not a poison!"
"No, but one drop and you're dead!"

75) "Waiter," said Dad, "please explain to me why there are footprints in my food."
"Well," said the waiter, "you rushed in, asked for a large omelet and told me to step on it!"

76) "The teacher said I could play in the school soccer team if it weren't for two things," said Frances. "What two things?" asked Dad.
"My feet," said Frances.

77) "How much is a soda?" Dad asked the store assistant.
Two dollars," she said. "And how much is a refill?" asked Dad. "The refill is free," said the assistant.
"Well then," said Dad, "I'll take the refill."

78) At dinner time, Joshua pushed away his plate.

"I don't like this cheese with holes in it," he grumbled.

"Well just eat the cheese and leave the holes on the side of your plate," said Dad.

79) "Would you like a pocket calculator for your birthday?" Dad asked Henry.

"No thanks, Dad," said Henry.

"I already know how many pockets I have."

80) "When I was your age, I wanted to be a garbage collector," said Dad. "Do you need any experience to do that job?" asked Oscar.

"No, I just picked it up as I went along."

81) "What do really clever children have for lunch?" asked Dad.

"I don't know," said his son.

"Hmm, no. I didn't think you would."

82) "Did you hear the joke about the rope, Dad?" asked Jane.

"No, I don't think I know that one,"

"Oh, skip it!" sighed Jane.

83) Dad went to see the doctor.

"Doctor, Doctor," he said. "A crab just pinched my toe."

"Which one?" asked the doctor.

"I don't know, all crabs look the same to me."

84) "I know a joke about a runny nose," said Dad.

"Go on," said Mary, "tell me, then."

"Oh no," said Dad, "I've blown it again.

85) "Do gooseberries have legs?" asked Dad. "No," said Mom.

"Ah, then I've just swallowed a caterpillar."

86) "You should wash your face," said Dad to George.

"I can see what you had for breakfast today."

"Do you think so?" said George.

"Go on – tell me what I had for breakfast today."

"Oatmeal," said Dad.

"Wrong!" said George. "That's what I had for breakfast yesterday."

87) "Peter," said Dad, "why is there a mouse in your bath?"

"Because you told me to get squeaky clean!" said Peter.

88) Evie was doing her history homework. "Dad," she said, "When was Rome built?

Do you think it was built at night?"

"What makes you think that?" asked Dad.

"Well, Mom always says that Rome wasn't built in a day."

Chapter 3 - Wordplay Jokes

"My father didn't tell me how to live. He lived and let me watch him do it." ~ Clarence B Kelland

1) How can you double your money?

By folding the bills in half.

2) Why was the broom late?

Because he over swept.

3) What vegetable can sometimes be found in the bathroom sink?

A leek.

4) What smells, runs around all day and lies around with their tongues hanging out?

A pair of sneakers!

5) "I've just had to make an appointment for the dentist," said Dad.

"What time's your appointment?" asked Mom.

"Tooth hurty!"

6) Why was Daddy Rabbit so upset?

He was having a bad hare day.

7) Daddy Orange looked a little pale.

"I think I'd better go to the doctor," he groaned. "I'm not peeling well."

8) "Ned, please don't chew with your mouth open," said Mommy Horse.

"Yes, son," added Daddy Horse. "You really have bad stable manners."

9) Will you come out and play with me, Papa?" asked the Baby Sloth.
"Give me five minutes, said Papa. "I just want to finish my snooze paper."

10) Daddy Tomato was out for a run with his son.
"Come on, Son," he said. "Ketchup!"

11) "This boat trip is fun," said Mommy, "but what's all that meat in the water?"
"I don't know for sure," said Daddy, "but it's a bit choppy, isn't it?"

12) "Ouch!" said Mom. I've just cut my finger, chopping cheese.
"I think you may have grater problems," said Dad.

13) "Hey kids," said Dad.

"I've just swapped the bed where Mom and I sleep for a trampoline.

Don't tell Mom, though – she'll hit the roof!"

14) "I can't stand jokes about perforated paper," my Dad told me. "They're tearable."

15) "I was going to give you a big kiss," said Dad, "but you have a runny nose.

You may think it's funny, but it's snot."

16) Dad and Ella were out shopping.

"Look!" said Ella. "There's a special offer on at the pet shop this week."

"What is it?" asked Dad. "Buy a cat, get one flea?"

17) Who is the world's greatest underwater secret agent?

James Pond

18) Why are fish so clever?

They live in schools.

19) "Dad! Dad! What do you call a man with a car on his head?" said Andy.

"Jack!"

20) What's a toad's favorite drink?

- Croak-a cola!

21) Why couldn't the 101 dalmatians hide?

Because they'd already been spotted!

22) What do you call a Roman emperor with a cold?

Julius Sneezer!

23) How do you make a Mexican chilli?

Send him to the North Pole.

24) What's brown, sounds like a bell and comes out of a cow backwards?

DUNG!

25) Why did the frog take the bus to work?

His car got toad.

26) Why do you need to be careful when it's raining cats and dogs?

You might step in a poodle!

27) What's worse than raining cats and dogs?

Raining cabs!

28) Why do cats have bad breath?

They use mouse-wash!

29) What do you call a dinosaur fart?

A blast from the past!

30) What do you call a dinosaur that wears glasses?

A Doyouthinkysaurus!

31) Why did the poor frog travel along the freeway when his car broke down?

He waited hours to be toad away.

32) Which two days start with the letter 'T'?" asked the teacher.

"That's easy!" said Callum. "'Today' and 'Tomorrow'!"

33) Sharon and her dad were walking through town. "Where do you think that one-handed man is going?" wondered Sharon.

"To the second-hand shop!" said Dad.

34) There was once a wooden truck with wooden wheels and wooden seats. Why is it not moving?

The only problem was... it wooden go.

35) "When I grow up," said Amelia, "I want to drive a dustcart."

"Well I definitely won't stand in your way," said Dad.

36) "Dad," said Josh, "I was wondering if King Arthur ever had bad dreams?

"Yes, son: knight-mares."

37) "Hey Harriet," said Dad. "I sat up all night wondering where the sun had gone.

Then it dawned on me!"

38) How do you communicate with a fish?

Drop him a line.

39) Why did the winning soccer team spin their trophy round and round?

It was the Whirled Cup.

40) Why did the footballer play in his kitchen?

It was a home game.

41) Why did the boy eat his computer?

Because it was an Apple.

42) What do farmers give their wives on Valentine's Day?

Hogs and kisses.

43) How was the Roman Empire divided in two?

With a pair of caesars.

44) What's a sailor's favorite snack?

Chocolate ship cookies.

45) Why is money called dough?

Because we all knead it.

46) What did the earwig say when he fell off the twig?

'Ear wigo!

47) What do you get if you cross a chicken with a guitar?

A hen that makes music when you pluck it!

48) What do you get when you put three ducks into a carton?

A box of quackers.

49) What do you get when you cross a dinosaur with a grapefruit?

A dino-sour.

50) What do you call a dinosaur who is always walking in the mud?

A brown-toe-saurus.

51) What do you call a dinosaur that never gives up?

A try-try-try-ceratops.

52) Where do you find giant snails?

On the end of a giant's fingers.

53) Where is Timbuktu located?

Between Timbuk-one and Timbuk-three

54) "I've accidentally swallowed a dictionary," said Alex.

"Don't breathe a word of it to anybody," said Dad.

55) Why did James refuse to fix dinner for his family?

He didn't know it was broken

56) Dad had eaten one plate of pasta too many.

"I've gone pasta point of no return," he said.

57) What's gray, carries a bunch of flowers and makes you feel better when you're ill?

A get-wellephant.

58) What do you give to a lemon when it needs help?

Lemon-aid.

59) Which sport do horses like best?

Stable tennis.

60) What sort of tuba can't you play?

A tuba toothpaste.

61) Why did the witch keep turning into Minnie Mouse?

Because she had so many Disney spells.

62) How do chickens stay in shape?

The eggsercise.

63) What games do cannibals play?

Swallow the leader.

64) What's green with red spots?

A frog with chicken pox.

65) What's worse than an elephant with a sore trunk?

A centipede with sore feet.

66) Why did the porcupine say "Ouch! Ouch!"?

Because he put his coat on inside out.

67) What do you call a whale band?

An orca-stra.

68) Why did the antelope lose every card game he played?

Because he was playing with a cheetah.

69) How many insects do you need to fill an apartment block?

Tenants.

70) What do you get if you cross a toad with a galaxy?

Star warts.

71) What did one angel say to another angel?

"Halo there!"

72) Why did the daddy flea lose his job?

He wasn't up to scratch.

73) What sort of beans do monsters like to eat best of all?

Human beans.

74) When is the best time to buy budgies?

When they're going cheep.

75) What type of shoes do frogs wear?

Open toad sandals.

76) Where do ponies go when they're ill?

The horse-pital.

77) What do elephants do in the evenings?

They watch elevision.

78) What fruit never gets lonely?

A pear.

79) Why is there a "d" in bandana?

Because if there wasn't, pirates would be wearing bananas on their heads.

80) What happens if you cross a laptop with an elephant?

You get loads of memory, but your laptop will be too heavy to lift!

81) What's the worst thing about being an octopus?

Washing your hands before dinner.

82) What did Cinderella wear to go swimming?

Glass flippers.

83) What kind of ship never sinks?

A friendship.

84) How do aliens pass the time on long journeys?

They play astronauts and crosses.

85) Why did the boy ask his father to sit in the fridge?

He wanted an ice-cold pop.

86) What did one elevator say to the other elevator?

I think I'm coming down with something.

87) What do porcupines say after they kiss?

Ouch!

88) How do sheep get their hair cut?

They go to the baa-baas.

89) What is the biggest ant in the world?

An eleph-ant.

90) What did the mommy volcano say to the baby volcano?

"I lava you."

91) How do you know how much a sheep costs?

You scan its baa code!

92) What kind of pets just lie around the room?

Car-pets.

93) What musical instrument could be used for fishing?

A cast-a-net

Chapter 4: Knock-Knock Jokes

"One of the greatest things a father can do for his children is to love their mother." ~ Howard W Hunter

1) Knock Knock!

Who's there?

Cowgo

Cowgo who?

No, cow go moo!

2) Knock Knock

Who's there?

Cargo

Cargo who?

Cargo beep beep!

3) Knock Knock

Who's there?

Doctor

Doctor who?

Doctor Who and the Daleks!

4) Knock knock!

Who's there?

Luke.

Luke who?

Luke through the keyhole and you'll soon see that it's me!

5) Knock knock!

Who's there?

Amy.

Amy who?

Amy fraid I've locked myself out!

6) Knock knock!

Who's there?

Boo.

Boo who?

Don't cry – I'll let you in!

7) **Knock knock!**

Who's there?

A Tish

A Tish who?

Bless you!

8) **Knock knock!**

Who's there?

Bin.

Bin who?

Bin anywhere nice on your holidays?

9) Knock Knock!

Who's there?

Interrupting sheep.

Interupting she--

Baaaaaaaaaaah!

10) Knock knock!

Who's there?

Snot.

Snot who?

Snot fair – I don't have a key!

11) Knock knock!

Who's there?

Yah!

Yah who?

Ride 'em, cowboy!

12) Knock knock!

Who's there?

Juicy.

Juicy who?

Juicy that boy break your doorbell and run away?

13) Knock knock!

Who's there?

Justin.

Justin who?

Justin time for you to let me in!

14) Knock knock!

Who's there?

Abby.

Abby who?

Abby birthday to you, abby birthday to you...

15) Knock knock!

Who's there?

Canoe.

Canoe who?

Canoe come out and play today?

16) Knock knock!

Who's there?

Theodore.

Theodore who?

Theodore wasn't open so I knocked.

17) Knock knock!

Who's there?

General Lee.

General Lee who?

General Lee I rang your doorbell, but it wasn't working.

18) Knock knock!

Who's there?

Howard.

Howard who?

Howard you like to let me in?

19) Knock knock.

Who's there?

Kenya.

Kenya who?

Kenya think of a punchline for this joke?

20) Knock knock!

Who's there?

Six times seven is forteet

Six times seven is forteet who?

Wow! You're good at maths!

21) Knock knock

Who's there?

Frank

Frank who?

Frank you very much for reading these jokes!

One Final Thing...

Thank for making it through to the end of *The Try Not to Laugh Challenge: Joke Book: For Kids and Family Volume 1*, let's hope it was fun, challenging and able to provide you and your family with all of the entertainment you needed for this Easter day (raining or sunny afternoon)!

Did You Enjoy the Book?

If you did, please let us know by leaving a review on AMAZON. Review let Amazon know that we are creating quality material for children. Even a few words and ratings would go a long way. We would like to thank you in advance for your time.

If you have any comments, or suggestions for improvement for other books, we would love to hear from and you and can contact us at **riddleland@bmccpublishing.com**

Your comments are greatly valued, and the book have already been revised and improved as a result of helpful suggestions from readers.

Alert: Bonus Book for the Kids!

https://bit.ly/riddlelandbonus

Thank you for buying this book, We would like to share a special bonus as a token of appreciation. It is collection 50 original jokes, riddles and 2 funny stories

RIDDLES AND JOKES CONTESTS!!

Riddleland is having **2 contests** to see who are the smartest or funniest boys and girls in the world!

1) **Creative and Challenging Riddles**
2) **Tickle Your Funny Bone Contest**

Parents, please email us your child's "Original" Riddle or Joke **and he or she could win a $50 gift card to Amazon.**

Here are the rules:

7) It must be challenging for the riddles and funny for the jokes!

8) It must be 100% Original and not something from the internet! It is easy to find out!

9) You can submit both joke and riddle as they are 2 separate contests.

10)No help from the parents unless they are as funny as you.

11) Winners will be announced via email.

12)Email us at <u>Riddleland@bmccpublishing.com</u>

Other Fun Children Books For The Kids!

Riddles Series

Encourage your kids to think outside of the box

with these Fun and Creative Riddles!

Get them on Amazon!

Try Not to Laugh Challenge Series

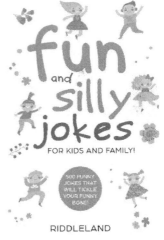

Get them on Amazon!

About the Author

Riddleland is a mom + dad run publishing company. We are passionate about creating fun and innovative books to help children develop their reading skill and fall in love with reading. If you have suggestions for us or want to work with us, shoot us an email at riddleland@bmccpublishing.com

Our family's favorite quote

"Creativity is area in which younger people have a tremendous advantage since they have an endearing habit of always questioning past wisdom and authority." – Bill Hewlett

Made in the USA
Columbia, SC
19 May 2019